KATHERINE SANTOS

# 101 THINGS
## EVERY KID NEEDS TO KNOW

From Chores to Social Skills

The content contained within this book may not be reproduced, duplicated or transmitted without direct written permission from the author or the publisher.

Under no circumstances will any blame or legal responsibility be held against the publisher, or author, for any damages, reparation, or monetary loss due to the information contained within this book. Either directly or indirectly. You are responsible for your own choices, actions, and results.

**Legal Notice:**

This book is copyright protected. This book is only for personal use. You cannot amend, distribute, sell, use, quote or paraphrase any part, or the content within this book, without the consent of the author or publisher.

**Disclaimer Notice:**

Please note the information contained within this document is for educational and entertainment purposes only. All effort has been executed to present accurate, up to date, and reliable, complete information. No warranties of any kind are declared or implied. Readers acknowledge that the author is not engaging in the rendering of legal, financial, medical or professional advice. The content within this book has been derived from various sources. Please consult a licensed professional before attempting any techniques outlined in this book.

By reading this document, the reader agrees that under no circumstances is the author responsible for any losses, direct or indirect, which are incurred as a result of the use of the information contained within this document, including, but not limited to, errors, omissions, or inaccuracies.

© Copyright 2024 - All rights reserved.

# TABLE OF CONTENT

**Becoming Self-Sufficient:**.................................................... **5**
    1. Cooking Simple Meals........................................................ 5
    2. Using Kitchen Appliances Safely....................................... 5
    3. Sewing and Mending........................................................ 6
    4. Doing Laundry.................................................................. 7
    5. Washing Dishes............................................................... 8
    6. Cleaning the House.......................................................... 8
    7. Gardening and Growing Plants........................................ 9
    8. Making Basic Repairs......................................................10
    9. Studying Independently................................................. 11
    10. Managing Your Schedule............................................. 12
    11. Taking on New Challenges........................................... 13
**Getting Along with Others:**................................................ **14**
    12. Positive Relationships with Family, Friends, and Classmates................................................................... 14
    13. Respecting Elders.........................................................15
    14. Learning from Parents and Guardians........................ 16
    15. Taking Responsibility for Your Actions........................ 17
    16. Practicing Patience and Understanding...................... 18
    17. Enjoying Outings With Loved Ones:............................ 19
    18. Keeping Yourself and Family Safe............................... 20
**Social Skills:**........................................................................ **22**
    19. Making Eye Contact..................................................... 22
    20. Using Good Manners................................................... 23
    21. Greeting People with Handshakes.............................. 24
    22. Apologizing When Necessary.......................................25
    23. Adapting to Changes in Plans..................................... 26
    24. Responding to Bullying................................................ 27
**Health and Wellness:**........................................................ **28**

25. Exercising..................................................................28
26. Limiting Screen Time................................................ 29
27. Making New Friends................................................ 30
28. Maintaining Good Friendships.................................. 30
29. Setting Healthy Boundaries...................................... 31
30. Eating Nutritious Foods........................................... 32
31. Practicing Good Hygiene......................................... 33
32. Building Confidence and Self-Esteem......................34
33. Talking with Your Doctor.........................................35
34. Getting Enough Sleep.............................................36
35. Avoiding Allergens.................................................. 36
36. Staying Safe...........................................................37
37. Being Prepared on the Go......................................38

**Recreation and Hobbies:.............................................. 40**
38. Trying New Activities.............................................. 40
39. Joining a Sports Team............................................41
40. Sticking with Rewarding Pastimes..........................41
41. Reading for Pleasure..............................................42
42. Biking and Skating Safely....................................... 43
43. Fishing and Hunting............................................... 44
44. Making and Enjoying Music....................................45
45. Expressing Creativity..............................................46

**Planning for the Future:............................................... 48**
46. Managing Money Wisely.........................................48
47. Disagreeing Politely................................................49
48. Accepting Constructive Feedback........................... 50
49. Knowing When to Ask for Help................................51
50. Writing Letters........................................................ 52
51. Emailing Formally...................................................53
52. Mailing Packages Properly..................................... 54
53. Giving Correct Change........................................... 55
54. Saying No to Harmful Activities............................... 56

55. Coping with Setbacks.................................................................57
56. Staying Resilient When Things Go Wrong............................. 58
57. Standing Up for Others............................................................ 59
58. Taking Responsibility.............................................................. 60
59. Caring for Pets.........................................................................61
60. Using the Internet Safely.........................................................62
61. Staying Safe Around Strangers................................................ 63
62. Using Proper Grammar............................................................ 64

**Being a Positive Influence..............................................................66**
63. Channeling Personal Hardships into Helping Others...........66
64. Seeing Other Perspectives.......................................................67
65. Admitting When You're Wrong................................................ 68
66. Becoming More Accepting of Differences.......................... 69
67. Comforting Others in Need......................................................70

**Doing Well in School:................................................................... 72**
68. Studying Efficiently.................................................................. 72
69. Getting Along with Teachers................................................... 73
70. Avoiding Gossip.......................................................................74
71. Knowing When to Get Involved............................................. 75
72. Improving Your Focus............................................................. 76
73. Working on Difficult Subjects................................................. 77
74. Retaining What You Learn...................................................... 78
75. Earning Good Grades.............................................................. 79
76. Speaking Confidently in Class................................................ 81
77. Coping with Sadness and Loss............................................... 82
78. Completing Assignments Honestly......................................... 83
79. Understanding Plagiarism....................................................... 84

**Working Outdoors Safely:..............................................................86**
80. Washing Cars Properly............................................................86
81. Maintaining Vehicles...............................................................87
82. Practicing Safety Around Cars................................................ 88
83. Mowing Lawns Correctly........................................................ 89

- 84. Handling Automotive Fluids Carefully.................................. 90
- 85. Identifying Dangerous Snakes.........................................91
- 86. Identifying Poisonous Plants..........................................93
- 87. Staying Safe in Bad Weather......................................... 94
- 88. Using Radios in Emergencies......................................... 95
- 89. Reading Maps..............................................................96
- 90. Asking for Directions Safely........................................... 97

**Appearance and Hygiene:................................................... 99**
- 91. Caring for Your Hair......................................................99
- 92. Styling Your Hair........................................................100
- 93. Planning Outfits.........................................................101
- 94. Caring for Your Skin.................................................. 102
- 95. Using Sun Protection................................................. 103
- 96. Dressing Appropriately.............................................. 104
- 97. Ironing Clothes......................................................... 106
- 98. Finding Personal Style............................................... 107
- 99. Brushing and Flossing Teeth...................................... 108
- 100. Feeling Good about How You Look............................ 109
- 101. Building Confidence in Yourself................................. 111

**ABOUT THE AUTHOR.........................................................113**

# Becoming Self-Sufficient:

## 1. Cooking Simple Meals

Learning to cook simple, nutritious meals is an essential life skill. Start with basic recipes like scrambled eggs, pasta, rice, roasted vegetables, salads, and sandwiches. Learn about kitchen safety, using knives properly, avoiding cross-contamination, and not leaving food out too long. Help children gain confidence by allowing them to select recipes, purchase ingredients, and take the lead in preparing dishes. Teach them to read a recipe, gather materials, prep ingredients, use appliances safely, follow cooking directions carefully, and ask for assistance when needed. Clean up together afterwards.

## 2. Using Kitchen Appliances Safely

The kitchen contains potentially dangerous appliances and tools. Children should receive full instructions and close supervision when using items like stoves, ovens, microwaves, blenders, mixers, knives, and more. Explain the proper procedures for turning appliances on and off, handling hot dishes, opening/closing doors, inserting/removing food items, using timers and controls, unplugging devices, allowing cooling time, and wiping up spills right away. Reinforce safe practices through patient modeling and practice. Check regularly for understanding.

## *3. Sewing and Mending*

Basic sewing skills allow one to repair torn clothing and create simple projects. Select child-safe fabric scissors, needles, pins, thread, sewing machine, iron, and measuring tape. Demonstrate hand-sewing techniques like basting, running stitch, backstitch, hemming, and patching holes. For machine sewing, show threading, winding bobbins, selecting stitches, guiding fabric, and changing needle positions. Start with things like pillows, totes, blankets, or stuffed animals.

Provide close guidance as they practice. Displaying finished items boosts pride and motivation!

## 4. Doing Laundry

Around ages 8-12, most kids possess the coordination and responsibility to tackle laundry tasks. Break down steps like sorting colors/whites, choosing cycles/temperatures, measuring detergent, treating stains, loading machines properly, adding fabric softener, drying items completely, folding neatly, and putting away clothing. Clear labeling, storage, and reminders help cement routines. Praise progress and allow natural consequences for forgetting loads. Share your systems for organizing laundry on busy mornings. Doing one's own laundry promotes competence and self-reliance!

## 5. Washing Dishes

Hand washing dishes builds character! Demonstrate proper use of dish soap, sponges, hot rinse water, dish racks for drying, and storage locations for cleaned items. Explain careful handling of breakables. Have children clear table spaces after meals and carefully scrape and rinse dishes before soaking to remove debris. Show circular scrubbing action. Define "water-spotting" on glassware. Discuss food safety issues like separating cutting boards, sanitizing countertops, avoiding germ-spreading dishcloths, and taking out trash right away. Make a game of racing to finish. Offer to trade off washing/drying tasks.

## 6. Cleaning the House

Maintaining tidy home environments requires regular upkeep but teaches organization, time management, efficiency, and responsibility. Around age 10, guide children through basic housekeeping like making beds, putting away belongings, vacuuming, dusting, cleaning sinks/counters, scrubbing bathrooms, mopping, waste disposal, recycling, and yard work. Create checklists of rotating chores. Demonstrate proper usage of cleaning products and caution about combinations. Schedule regular decluttering sessions. Share energy-saving habits like turning off lights. Offer rewards for extra initiative like washing windows or baseboards!

## 7. Gardening and Growing Plants

Connecting with nature brings immense satisfaction. Nurture love for the environment by involving kids in lawn/garden care. Review safety rules for yard tools and chemicals. Demonstrate proper use of hoses, pruners, rakes, shovels, and wheelbarrows. Teach them to weed, edge, sweep walkways, tend compost piles, and clean gutters. Show how to prepare soil, select hardy plants, space rows, sow seeds at proper depths, set out transplants, use row covers/cages, water appropriately, fertilize if needed, and protect buds from frost. Let them sample edible flowers and herbs. Have them journal observations as vegetables ripen or butterflies visit!

## 8. Making Basic Repairs

Over time, possessions break or fail. Rather than immediately replace items, teach kids to try fixing them first. Supply a toolbox with age-appropriate tools like screwdrivers, wrenches, tape, glues, safety gear, and headlamps. Start by having them reattach loose parts, tighten screws, patch holes with plaster, replace dead batteries or light bulbs, lubricate sticky mechanisms like cabinet hinges/bike chains/door knobs, update software drivers, troubleshoot wiring faults, reprogram controls, or splice damaged cords. Reward resourcefulness and celebrate hard-earned fixes! Advanced learners can assemble new purchases requiring assembly. The ability to make repairs saves money and reduces waste.

## 9. Studying Independently

Self-directed learning habits pave the way for academic and career success. Around fourth grade, children possess sufficient focus to manage 30-90 minutes of independent daily studying. Guide them to set intentions for study sessions, break assignments into chunks, create task checklists, assemble materials, eliminate distractions, take breaks as needed, ask clarifying questions, restate main ideas, and reward progress. Teach effective strategies like summarization, mnemonic devices, visual aids, note-taking, timelines, and recitation. Show them how to set study reminders, track assignments on calendars, plan long-term projects, and self-test retention before exams. Help them identify topics warranting tutoring. Monitoring their own progress fosters agency and work ethic.

## 10. Managing Your Schedule

Juggling school, activities, chores and social events - plus enough free time just to play or relax - challenges children's organizational skills. Sit down together and map out typical weekly routines hour by hour. Estimate homework/study requirements. Block fixed activities like sports practice or music lessons. Add household responsibilities, errands or part-time jobs. Allow spaces for meals, hygiene, family time and open-ended recreation or hobbies. Refer often to the master calendar and have kids enter reminders themselves. If schedules overwhelm, discuss scaling back obligations. Demonstrate tools and apps to track tasks, set alerts before transitions, build prep time into mornings or carry checklists. Review what worked and what felt stressful each week, adjusting as needed.

## *11. Taking on New Challenges*

Pushing past comfort zones helps young people unlock grit, resilience, confidence and skills. Notice areas where children avoid risk, struggle with change or limit themselves. Perhaps they decline school leadership roles, avoid competitive teams, won't attempt advanced math or hesitate mingling at social events. Ask them about their hesitations. Brainstorm incremental steps to challenge those boundaries, ensuring adequate support structures are in place. The simple act of public speaking might progress from reading poetry aloud with family to presenting full speeches to audiences. Use encouragement and small successes to tackle progressively tougher challenges related to health, creativity, athletics or academics. Meet them where they are and celebrate each attempt at self-improvement!

# Getting Along with Others:

## 12. Positive Relationships with Family, Friends, and Classmates

Learning to build strong interpersonal relationships increases quality of life. Coach children to show genuine interest in others, ask questions, listen fully, emphasize shared priorities, validate different perspectives, communicate needs/boundaries, and speak using "I feel" statements during conflicts. Role model healthy dynamics through open affection, shared activities, accountability and apologies within your family. Support their friendships by welcoming guests, driving respectfully when carpooling, and monitoring online interactions. Advocate for kindness by reporting bullying when warranted. Discuss balancing one-on-one time vs group activities. Explore personality tests together to appreciate differences. Share your own stories of how relatives, friends or mentors impacted your life.

## 13. Respecting Elders

In many cultures, elders represent treasured sources of wisdom gained through decades of experiences. Yet industrialized societies often isolate seniors. Instilling respect across generations brings mutual benefits. Engage kids and older relatives in oral history interviews. Ask elders to teach hands-on skills like cooking family recipes, woodworking or folk music. Schedule visits to senior centers to socialize. Assist neighbors by raking leaves, shoveling snow or delivering groceries when mobility becomes limited. Discuss ageist assumptions as you encounter them. Challenge underrepresentation of seniors in media and advertising. Learn about the physical realities of aging to increase empathy. Participate in "adopt a grandparent" programs through schools or churches. Valuing elder perspectives reminds all ages of our shared human dignity.

## 14. Learning from Parents and Guardians

The most enduring life lessons stem from primary caregivers. Make space for teachable moments as you move through daily routines together. Narrate thought processes while prepping meals, balancing budgets, completing repairs, resolving conflicts or helping others in need. Answer endless questions about the world patiently. Instill family or cultural values through stories, celebrations and volunteer work. Share favorite books/films from your childhood, play classic games, or attempt hobbies you once enjoyed like painting, chess or stargazing. Pass along specialized skills like athletic techniques, musical instruments or trade skills gained from your own upbringing. Ask their input about household decisions to encourage critical thinking. Children integrate these family experiences into their blossoming identities.

## 15. Taking Responsibility for Your Actions

Accountability builds integrity. Children mature greatly when held responsible for their choices proportionate to age/ability without undue harshness. Build awareness of how words/behaviors impact others. Give them chances to make minor decisions independently, even if they choose poorly at first. Resist rescuing too quickly. Let small failures provide learning experiences, then offer support. Follow any natural/logical consequences of ignoring warnings. If they break dishes while roughhousing indoors after cautions, expect them to pay for replacements from savings. Stress making amends through apologies, changed behaviors and restitution. Praise efforts to admit mistakes and think through "what if" alternative choices when incidents occur. Taking responsibility marks the transition from childhood into emerging adulthood.

## *16. Practicing Patience and Understanding*

Fast-paced environments and constant stimulation make patience and interpersonal insight rare virtues nowadays. Yet the ability to compassionately "read" varied situations and respond thoughtfully may prove more valuable than academic or technical prowess. Nurture empathy through literature exploring hardships faced by different groups throughout history. Discuss examples of patience and mercy. Role model calm responses, even when frustrated. Admit your own difficulties in this area and share what helps you demonstrate self-restraint. Praise small acts of consideration, compromise and conflict resolution between siblings or classmates. Volunteer serving vulnerable community members to expand perspectives. Choose understanding over reactions as a family by taking deep breaths, listening fully and reserving judgments.

## *17. Enjoying Outings With Loved Ones:*

Quality time adventuring together fortifies family bonds forging treasured memories spanning generations. Choose excursions suiting relatives' varied interests, activity levels and budgets to spark meaningful conversations. Splurge on annual vacations within driving distance like campgrounds, amusement parks, cultural festivals, historical sites, national parks or beach trips. Scout mobility assistance and interpretive services in advance if applicable. Preview attractions online, noting admission/parking/food costs and crowd levels expecting wheelchair space for optimal experiences. Along the journey, sing favorite tunes or attempt regional accents while posing silly at roadside oddity stops!

During simpler weekend days, revisit nostalgic dating spots from parents' early years, hit disc golf courses, volunteer at animal shelters, wander downtown boutiques, create scavenger hunts at museums, geocache nearby nature preserves or cheer at community theater productions. Pack comfortable walking shoes, water bottles, sun protection and jackets for changing conditions. Share favorite family stories over picnic meals or post-adventure hot chocolates. City dwellers can find escapes biking greenbelt trails ending in ice cream shops or stargazing rural sunset vistas from tailgate tents. Wherever you explore together, prioritize true connections over jam-packed sightseeing. After all, families already include ultimate travel companions for making memories.

## 18. Keeping Yourself and Family Safe

As members of a household, each person contributes to collective security and preparedness. Review emergency protocols like fire escape routes and storm shelter plans until everyone memorizes details. Ensure properly functioning smoke detectors, fire extinguishers and first aid kits. Lock doors/windows and activate alarms every night.

Share itineraries/contact info when individuals travel separately. Sign up for community alert systems regarding weather or public threats. Learn basic self-defense and first aid techniques at local workshops. Prominently post poison control and domestic violence hotlines. Set and enforce reasonable curfews based on age and maturity during free time. Discuss actions to take when witnessing crimes or approaches by strangers exhibiting troubling behaviors either in public spaces or online. Establishing prudent safeguards can save lives.

# Social Skills:

## 19. Making Eye Contact

Direct eye contact demonstrates confidence, trustworthiness and engagement during interactions. Yet some cultures discourage prolonged stares. Teach appropriate levels of eye contact through modeling and practice. Have children look closely at their own eye colors, creases and lashes in a mirror to become comfortable with faces. Practice maintaining gaze while conversing, listening or shaking hands. Count slowly to 5-7 seconds at a time. Praise steady glance exchanges. Describe how eyes convey emotions like joy, sadness and anger. Demonstrate glancing away periodically before returning focus as a sign of respect. Role play situations like introductions, expressing thanks, making requests or apologizing while incorporating proper eye contact. Remind them to blink frequently to remain approachable. Making eye contact at suitable moments strengthens connections.

## 20. Using Good Manners

Well-mannered children mature into gracious adults respected by peers. Etiquette provides guidelines, not hard rules, that evolve across generations and settings. Demonstrate table manners like subtle closed-mouth chewing with utensils, dabbing mouths before drinking, and passing dishes politely. Expect "please" and "thank you" phrases reflexively. Discuss courteous online communications without teasing or all-caps. Role model kind language even when angry. Before play dates, talk through respecting each other's homes and toys. Provide gentle corrections privately if needed. Explain manners and show others they matter. Emphasize inclusiveness at gatherings. Treat service staff exceptionally well. Doing small things to put others at ease makes the world friendlier.

## 21. Greeting People with Handshakes

Handshakes establish rapport, especially between children and adults or when making introductions. Demonstrate extending the right hand promptly while standing an arm's length apart and making eye contact. Show a firm but not crushing grip for 2-3 seconds while lightly pumping up and down once or twice. Explaining this conveys respect, trust and focus. Help timid children rehearse approaches, self-introductions and smiles without staring at their feet. Remind them dry palms prevent slippery handshakes. Use gentle humor if overly anxious. Praise progress interacting formally or when remembering relatives' preferred left-handed greetings. Compliment genuine expressions and clear voices while mingling at gatherings. Confidence in greeting elders, peers and community members brings lifelong connections.

## 22. Apologizing When Necessary

Heartfelt apologies heal relationships after conflicts or harm. Explain admitting mistakes with sincerity and remorse demonstrates courage and accountability. Discuss examples of small slights and proportional responses to situations necessitating extensive amends. Demonstrate wording like "I apologize for my actions. I understand they caused you pain. You didn't deserve that. In the future I will think before acting. Please forgive me in time." Remind children apologies focus on impacts to others rather than justifications for misbehaviors. Have them rehearse empathy by writing apology letters as if they are bullies, characters from books or news figures before discussing as a family why certain actions require true change. Naming potential consequences helps guide moral reasoning and integrity.

## 23. Adapting to Changes in Plans

Resilience develops through experiencing occasional disappointments when well-supported. Schedules shift constantly as life unfolds unexpectedly. Seize these moments to bolster coping abilities. Praise flexibility during mundane inconveniences like delayed mealtimes or switching activities. Validate feelings after special event cancellations. Ask curious questions about possible reasons behind changes. Demonstrate reorganizing logistics spontaneously, then refocusing attention on present moments. Share stories about your own growth through adapted plans. Guide kids to practice regulating frustration and see possibilities rather than losing inner balance. Carpool detours make space for meaningful conversations. Rainy campouts become cozy fort building sessions. Foster attitudes embracing life's unfolding surprises!

## 24. Responding to Bullying

Cruel teasing, harassment or manipulation harms all involved. Validate children's discomfort immediately if sharing about bullying. Report behaviors to appropriate authorities, even minor incidents, to establish records if patterns exist. Discuss realistic intervention options and assertiveness strategies like the "broken record" technique of calmly repeating statements rejecting intolerable behaviors. Encourage befriending isolated peers. Challenge restrictions on gender expressions during free play. Interrupt cruel jokes immediately; explain why remarks prove harmful. If bullying continues over staff objections, enroll children in empowerment training like martial arts, creative arts therapy or social justice youth leadership programs building confidence and broader social circles. Establish no-tolerance family policies against all bigotry. Cultivating compassion and courage through guidance thwarts bullying.

# Health and Wellness:

## 25. Exercising

Regular physical activity boosts mood, sleep, focus and heart health for kids of all athletic abilities. Explore preferences like team sports, solo pastimes, outdoor adventures or recreational leagues to discover lifelong fitness habits. Demonstrate use of home exercise equipment, walking/bike trails and community centers. Try new activities together as a family. Discuss healthy competition vs overtraining risks. Set incremental goals for strength, flexibility and endurance. Applaud genuine effort over innate talent. Share tips for injury prevention, hydration, nutritious protein intake, social connection and mindfulness about all body types having value and dignity. Establish screen-free bedrooms and household policies limiting sedentary time. Exercise feels rewarding when framed as an act of self-care rather than a chore.

## 26. Limiting Screen Time

While technology connects and entertains, excessive digital immersion carries risks spanning from mental health to online safety threats, especially for developing brains. Set clear boundaries on recreational screen usage based on age, tying access to completion of responsibilities first. Encourage offline hobbies and social interactions. Charge devices overnight outside bedrooms for better sleep. Model putting phones away to fully engage with kids during conversations. Set tech-free times family-wide. Use apps like "Moment" to track total hours spent on games, videos or social media. For children exceeding agreed upon limits, have them set their own alarms or use timers permitting short bouts only. Offer ample warning before time expires. Discuss online content together frequently to enforce internet safety.

## 27. Making New Friends

Social skills nurture community ties. Stretch comfort zones safely to increase self-confidence and support networks. Encourage attending diverse school events, recreational activities, summer camps, leadership programs and volunteer groups based on passions. Role model introductions with eye contact, handshakes and questions to prompt dialogue. Provide conversation prompts to help shy children open up at gatherings. Suggest exchanging contact information to solidify new bonds over shared interests. Look for chances to widen circles by hosting classmates for play dates or sleepovers. Friendships may spark anywhere if we release assumptions. Diversity brings growth for all involved.

## 28. Maintaining Good Friendships

Close companions provide affection, trust and assistance through life's journey. Nurture children's friendships between classmates, teammates, cousins or neighbors through reliability and empathy. Stress showing up on time when meeting up. Take turns choosing shared activities. Give space for inside jokes but curb excessive teasing. Discourage toxic bonding by excluding others. Express appreciation for kind gestures like consoling tears or defending your child from bullying. Remind kids that all humans experience hard times needing compassion. Support conflict resolution skills when disagreements inevitably occur. True friendships continue despite ups and downs. Prioritize treasured bonds as the years pass.

### 29. Setting Healthy Boundaries

Self-advocacy around personal rights and limitations preserves integrity. Discuss boundary-setting through examples like politely declining activities feeling unsafe, requesting friends avoid vulgar jokes, or budgeting playtime before chores. Describe consent or when to enlist support from responsible adults. Provide words to firmly reject inappropriate contact. Stress respecting others' stated boundaries in return. Repeat key phrases through role playing to directly address inappropriate behaviors or communication crossing lines: "Please stop commenting on my body." "I won't keep secrets from my parents." "Don't touch my private areas." Give opportunities to write/practice consent scripts until children can thoughtfully articulate boundaries feeling right for their developing stages. Honoring all people's personal agency establishes trust and strong relationships.

## 30. Eating Nutritious Foods

Lifelong healthy eating habits start early by making balanced selections automatic throughout each day. Involve children in meal planning/preparation using nutrition guidelines: Plenty vegetables, whole fruit, whole grains, plant-based proteins and healthy fats like olive oil or avocado instead of saturated fats; Moderate dairy, nuts, eggs, seafood, poultry and red meats rarely; Minimal processed snacks, juices and sweets for celebrations only. Discuss intuitive cues for hunger/fullness rather than emotions, boredom or food rewards/restrictions. Model positive attitudes towards nourishing foods over fad diets or negative body image crushing joy. Building nutrition literacy from a young age prevents many health issues ahead!

## 31. Practicing Good Hygiene

Instilling daily hygiene habits like bathing, oral care and grooming prevents illness while boosting confidence socially. Make routines fun rather than chore-like. Allow children age-appropriate independence assessing their own grooming needs, notice subtle peer pressures about appearance. Stock bathrooms with visual schedules/checklists, stools for shorter kids, non-slip mats and hygiene products suiting sensitive skin types if applicable. Set smartphone alerts so mature children remember to shower, brush teeth twice daily, apply deodorant, wash faces to prevent acne, trim nails and comb hair neatly. Compliment hygiene improvements verbally. Lead by example maintaining your own health standards. Most people focus more on personality than appearances!

## 32. Building Confidence and Self-Esteem

Positive self-regard unlocks potential by silencing inner critics seeking perfection. Build identity and purpose not contingent on achievements or others' validation. Nurture self-awareness of strengths and growth areas to leverage abilities fully. Allow mistakes as learning opportunities rather than embarrassment. Assign household roles promoting agency, like caring for pets or cooking. Share your own journey towards self-acceptance. Redirect negative body image or comparisons. Suggest writing affirmations, expanding diverse friend groups to find belonging and viewing obstacles as challenges to overcome.

Therapy aids some. Most importantly, expressing loving approval often does children internalize beloved worth beyond accomplishments.

## 33. Talking with Your Doctor

Doctors provide personalized medical advice to optimize wellness. Yet discussing health concerns feels vulnerable. Prepare children to participate actively in appointments. Explain patient confidentiality. Rehearse symptoms, family history and questions using friendly dolls. Schedule their own preventative checkups to ask directly about normal growth, nutrition, safe sex, mental health, drugs/alcohol and other age-related issues. Attend together initially if preferred, then step out periodically to build responsibility. Verify understanding of directions. Advise summarizing worries first when emotions overwhelm. Discuss recommendations privately after visits. Managing healthcare independently prevents delays getting needed treatment.

## 34. Getting Enough Sleep

Adequate sleep protects growing bodies and minds, enhancing memory, immunity and behavior regulation. Establish calming bedtime routines away from screens. Limit caffeinated beverages altogether for anxious children. Share favorite soothing songs/stories from when they were younger. Try weighted blankets, lavender eye pillows, guided meditations or back rubs to unwind tense muscles. Install blackout curtains and wake-up lights to encourage natural circadian rhythms. Record weekly rest totals to make needed adjustments. Implement earlier turn-in times before important academic performances. Watch for persistent fatigue signals like mood changes signaling potential underlying issues. Healthy sleep hygiene benefits people of all ages.

## 35. Avoiding Allergens

Allergies and asthma plague millions, especially children, threatening active lifestyles. Protect susceptible kids by identifying specific triggers through medical evaluations then minimizing exposures. Closely supervise young relatives when visiting homes with furry pets. Request school accommodations like nut-free cafeterias and asthma emergency plans. Swap air fresheners/fragrant soaps for natural cleansing products. Install quality filters on home ventilation systems. Schedule thorough seasonal cleanings removing dust-collecting clutter. Check pollen/air quality levels daily and choose indoor play if high. Recognize early signs of respiratory distress; adjust activities. Experiment to find antihistamines providing relief without drowsiness if over-the-counter medications are needed frequently. Stay vigilant!

## 36. Staying Safe

Safety consciousness minimizes preventable harm, especially around roads, water, medications or weapons. Supervise play near streets/parking lots. Model crossing at crosswalks and obeying traffic signals. Require bike helmets; teach hand signals. Around pools, lakes or beaches, actively watch young swimmers using U.S. Coast Guard-approved life jackets. Install latches on toxic products or firearms locked away from kids' access. Program poison control hotlines into cell phones and store ipecac syrup for inducement of vomiting if advised. Recognize abuse red flags like unexplained bruises, injuries or behaviors. Establish trusting open communication encouraging disclosure around bullying, unsafe touches or substances. Stay alert to surroundings when out together. Proactive precautions avoid tragedies.

## 37. Being Prepared on the Go

Confidently navigating the wider world prevents feeling overwhelmed by unexpected situations when running daily errands, enjoying vacations or facing detours. Maintain updated ID/medical cards and emergency contacts easily accessible in phones, wallets or bags. Pack tissues, bandages, pain/allergy medications and extra masks, hand sanitizer, snacks always. Review public transit routes online beforehand if complex. Download offline maps to avoid getting lost without cell signals. Carry cash for parking meters/pay phones and credit cards covering meals/hotels in emergencies. Check weather and pack layers adjusting for changes in forecast. Share real-time locations using phone apps when splitting up. Thinking ahead provides freedom to handle adventures!

# Recreation and Hobbies:

## 38. Trying New Activities

Sampling unique experiences outside everyday routines often sparks latent passions. Identify children's current interests across creative arts, sports, academics, crafts, technology, performance or service domains during family meetings. Explore enrichment opportunities in your region like summer camps focusing on everything from archaeology to zoology! Sign up for one-day workshops taught by visiting experts covering topics as diverse as stargazing, robotics and foreign languages. Check community center catalogs for affordable recreational classes. Strike up conversations with hobbyists you meet to learn about how they developed skills. Some kids thrive when selecting their own activities based on independence level. Trying new things flexes mental muscles while discovering joyful lifelong pursuits.

### 39. Joining a Sports Team

Beyond physical exercise and coordination, group athletics build social skills, outlet stress constructively and set foundations for healthy competition. Survey options like school teams, city recreational leagues, martial arts dojos, backyard clubs formed by neighborhood youth, swim associations or homeschool co-ops covering everything from acrobatics to fencing to Quidditch from the Harry Potter series! Attend try-outs together for moral support. Commit to regular practices and games. Model good sportsmanship win or lose. Volunteer to assist coaches or host end-of-season parties. Healthy athletic engagement teaches about emotional regulation, resilience, camaraderie, persistence and pride.

### 40. Sticking with Rewarding Pastimes

Consistency develops talents and passion. Nurture sustained engagement with activities feeling enjoyable first, without excessive pressure to excel. Facilitate access to gear and transportation for motivated interests. Help create practicing incentives like rewards grids. Ask curious questions about aspects warranting improvements to demonstrate support. Invest time bonding through participation, allowing children to share what sparks their enthusiasm. Troubleshoot barriers as they arise, like performance anxiety. Connect with others sharing the pastime to generate inspiration. Display mementos marking growth through the years. Whether arts, academics, athletics or hobby clubs, sticking with rewarding pastimes creates confidence to take on greater challenges ahead!

## 41. Reading for Pleasure

Reading imagination-firing novels builds vocabulary, empathy and mental sharpness. Make reading irresistible, not forced. Introduce compelling, age-appropriate series across genres featuring characters similar to your child's demographics. Create cozy spaces for independent reading or listening to audiobooks. Visiting libraries often allow kids to run free selecting their own materials. Demonstrate by example enjoying your own book while they read. Ask curious questions about unfolding plot lines from their chosen titles. Share family read-aloud time with animated voices or spooky flashlight stories. Gift books matching current passions on holidays. When kids associate reading with joy, skills improve subconsciously. A lifelong reader journeys anywhere.

## 42. Biking and Skating Safely

Pedaling miles or rolling smoothly on skates provides freeing transportation alternatives while building leg strength and stamina. Start safe habits early by modeling protective equipment for all riders like helmets meeting national safety standards, padding on knees/elbows, bright clothing and correct hand signals. Choose beginner trails or surfaces free from traffic allowing space to learn balance and stopping techniques. Customize bike seats/handlebars suiting kids' height. Consider enrolling in cycling education programs as skills progress. Praise efforts learning new tricks or biking places independently the green way. Maintain bikes and skates properly including inflation, lubrication, tightening loose parts that cause falls if neglected and replacing worn items as needed. Wheels equal freedom and confidence soaring!

## 43. *Fishing and Hunting*

Connecting with nature through hunting or fishing creates patient observers attuned to our role within ecosystems, following proper seasons and limits to find meals through self-reliant means. Verify completed hunter/boating safety courses for ages required in your state. Assemble essential gear like licenses, bait/ammunition, waders, special apparel to keep scent muted, sharpened knives, first aid kits, headlamps, backup chargers/radios/fire-starters and stray animal defense if warranted like bear spray. Scout sites in advance and purchase seasonal permits as needed. Set wake-up times respecting dawn patrols! Follow the rhythms of migrations, feeding and hibernation driving movement. Clean/cook any fare caught ethically. Pass along generations-old secrets so sustainable wildlife management thrives. The outdoors ground us.

## 44. Making and Enjoying Music

Whether musicians performing polished recitals or enthusiastic participants clapping along, immersing in music boosts creativity, literacy and academic performance from a young age. Survey instrument options matching kids' interests, dexterity and someday ensemble participation. Consider sound levels for apartment neighbors if drums get chosen! Cover rental fees if needed. Ask about favorite songs and genres to customize early playlists over family dance parties. Play ambient classical scores during homework time shown to aid concentration. Attend free community concerts at parks or marching competitions to appreciate diverse talents. Cheer proudly at school shows too. For reluctant singers, join group karaoke nights just for fun over special effects and costumes rather than judging skill. The world feels harmonious while celebrating music.

## 45. Expressing Creativity

Expressing Creativity through Arts Immersing in visual, written, music, dance or theatrical arts enriches young lives by channeling emotional experiences into positive self-discovery. Support creative bug bites when children gravitate towards instruments, easels, sewing machines or bookshelves instinctively. Invest in starter supplies and lessons within budget means like community center classes. Display finished pieces prominently in frames or performance videos on digital albums. Share your own amateur works to model lifelong learning rather than talent judgments.

When interest intensifies, help research application requirements for specialty high schools, museum workshops, youth karate troupes or summer writing intensives. Add mileage logging arts apprentice commutes into family schedules. Adapt spaces for rehearsal needs whether space to pirouette, sufficient wattage track lighting directing on nude figure studies, garage band noise barriers or basement theater sets under construction. Beyond technical skill-building, creative flow teaches vital emotional intelligence skills like innovative problem-solving, empathetic perspectives, resilience when critique stings, and confidence to boldly express minority voices through compelling activism mediums. Dreams manifest through arts immersion. What hidden gems await uncovered within their young spirits?

# Planning for the Future:

## 46. Managing Money Wisely

Financial literacy empowers responsible prioritizing, saving and sharing money earned through allowances, jobs or gifts. Open bank accounts together explaining balancing deposits/withdrawals, maintaining minimums to avoid fees, saving interest and online security. Create shared documents tallying income/expenses. Set give/save/spend allowance percentages or splits encouraging generosity. Assign bill-paying or comparison shopping tasks. Discuss needs vs wants when deciding bigger purchases and creating budgets with cushion room undoing overspending. Review terms like debt, credit, investing and compound interest across savings vehicles like CDs or IRAs. Foster delayed gratification for pricier goals. Check credit reports together before colleges or apartments affecting approval odds. Building money management abilities young prevents dependence and frees focus towards more rewarding priorities.

## 47. Disagreeing Politely

Conflicts arise routinely requiring civil discourse skills, especially surrounding ethics. As issues trigger emotions, model stabilizing tactics before continuing meaningful debates. Teach respectful questioning of opinions differing from family or faith norms instead of reactive judging. Frame larger societal dilemmas through historical context and data. Analyze molded biases. Discuss when to stand firm or compromise certain practices if causing harm unsupported by other credible evidence. Outline a code of conduct before contentious conversations such as no profanity, listening without interruption, right to pass on uncomfortable questions, recessing to regroup if tense. Agree on intended resolutions beforehand: Either simply share perspectives, find middle ground or change views. Societal progress flows from compassionate disagreement.

## 48. Accepting Constructive Feedback

Growing through critique deepens talents and ideas. Transparently share your own self-improvement efforts surrounding professional evaluations, creative works or athletic techniques as examples. Praise initial vulnerability receiving feedback. Suggest summarizing key points before reacting to demonstrate engaged listening and self-regulation even when assessments sting in the moment. Brainstorm next-step options: Acquire missing skills via classes or tutorials? Blind-test altered versions to gauge effectiveness? Survey trusted advisors contributing other insights if needed? Reframing mental scripts from victimhood towards empowerment models agency, as we cannot control outside opinions, just our responses. Converting feedback into fuel propelling growth takes practice and courage, but unlocks new horizons!

## 49. Knowing When to Ask for Help

Relying on others' wisdom reveals humanity's interdependence while preventing floundering through challenges alone. Instill comfort leveraging support. Distinguish situations benefiting from third party mediation, like teacher conferences when academics decline or therapists untangling volatile emotions exceeding family expertise. Role model including specialists ranging from car mechanics to IT consultants to interior designers when appropriate skill sets get surpassed by particular home projects. Phone trusted confidants when needing an empathetic ear. Practice scripts anonymously reporting risky peers, suspected neglect/abuse, or requesting crisis hotline contacts if reluctance overrides health. Portray help-seeking as prudent rather than weak. We all occasionally require guidance navigating life's many winding roads ahead. Community matters.

## 50. Writing Letters

Well-composed personal letters communicate caring across distances although increasingly rare in numbingly quick-reflex digital era tendencies. Consider reviving this thoughtful tradition to enhance emotional intelligence for young people weaned on emoji exchanges. Demonstrate addressing envelopes formally, crafting salutations/signoffs suiting relationships from thank you notes to pen pals, asking evocative questions in opening lines and injecting humor throughout anecdotes before signing with fountain pens adding vintage flair. Parse complex feelings through therapeutic journaling. Mail surprise paper packages to long-distance relatives using decorative washi tape. Send congratulatory cards for milestones when social media posts feel impersonal. Perfecting meaningful letter writing skills deepens connections in our isolated age.

## 51. Emailing Formally

As the internet facilitates global conversations instantly, students require proper digital communication etiquette aligned with professional norms they'll soon encounter entering careers. Ensure school email accounts activate safely without oversharing birthdays or locations. Review account security, strong password protection, and reporting suspicious activity. Compare reply-all uses and mass forwarding cautions. Stress signature lines on all messages, even brief replies, containing accurate name spellings, affiliation accuracy, contact information and mailing address protecting online privacy somewhat until personal trust builds. Triple check attachments and hyperlinks before clicking send. Finally, gently remind: Words posted electronically endure permanently impacting reputations and relationships despite damage control attempts. Censor snarky venting texts better whispered privately to BFFs instead!

## 52. Mailing Packages Properly

Navigating post office shipping proves mystifying with all those sticky forms and priority boxes, but mastering mail services saves money supporting entrepreneurs or faraway loved ones. Start practicing during easier summer breaks mailing care packages to homesick campers! Estimate weights by bathroom scale to prevent return fees. Wrap fragile goods securely, address legibly in center boxes avoiding edges that can tear and include return labels inside for unsuccessful delivery attempts. Lookup current pricing charts on the United States Postal Service website to calculate needed denominations for postage. Weigh packages prior to lining up so any adjustments occur before waiting turns frustrating. Kindly help older patrons perplexed by automated kiosks if you finish quickly. Mailing mishaps create headaches, but avoiding common mistakes smoothie sailing!

## 53. *Giving Correct Change*

Handling cash transactions ranks among essential functionality skills for maximal independence despite shifting digital payment preferences. Start practicing with reusable plastic fruits carts or play storefronts upgraded later towards teen roles as occasional grocery clerks, dog walkers paid by neighbors in cash or flea market sales booth managers. Master quickly tallying amounts, even long digit sums mentally, to prevent holding up lines. Double check totals avoiding register errors needing expensive refunds. Thank patrons for understanding honest mistakes. Keep currency/coins neatly sorted in compartments rather than digging through messy wallets and provide receipts for records. Giving correct change in various situations without reliance on technology proves a lifelong asset.

## 54. Saying No to Harmful Activities

Standing by personal boundaries despite negative peer pressure builds moral fortitude and self-preservation instincts. Discuss scenarios where students might feel nervous asserting needs, from sleepover activities feeling unsafe to refusing vapes or first-time alcohol. Validate discomfort confronting long term friends. Brainstorm polite refusal tactics like recommending alternative options everyone can participate in or pretending parents' house rules forbid participation. Convey unconditional support if lines get crossed, as prevention talks cannot control all behavior. Share relatable stories about times you declined risky things, partnerships voting differently. Requesting trusted teachers privately walks students away from impending trouble. Saying no at personal risk defines courageous character.

## 55. Coping with Setbacks

Resilience develops facing solvable setbacks through renewed perseverance rather than defeatism. Reframe reactions defining failures as lessons adjusting strategies towards eventual triumphs. When discouraged, inventory remaining strengths and supportive allies ready to reinforce comeback efforts, either emotionally or through skill-building. Maintain a balanced rational perspective about missteps typically proving insignificant years later, unlike compounding added regrets from abandoning aspirations due to single stumbles. Journal success stories of historical figures who overcame temporary obstacles through determined grit. Put preferred adversity coping mechanisms in place as convenient backups, from boxing frustration out at gyms to calming nature photography sessions so incremental progress continues forwards. This too shall pass with time.

## 56. Staying Resilient When Things Go Wrong

When inevitable chaos disrupts best laid plans, responding thoughtfully defines character. Model healthy emotional regulation rebooting optimism after miscarriages of justice from bad grades to championship losses. Validate disappointment initially but put time limits on sulking periods before regrouping. Prevent paralyzing anxious thoughts spiraling uncontrolled through worries list journaling, then shifting attention towards solutions-focused brainstorming. Is added studying, training or help needed moving on productively? Discuss coping strategies that restored your motivation after previous derailments. Reinforce taking reasonable responsibility where applicable but releasing fixating on unchangeable variables. Improvise memorable rituals celebrating resolved hardship experiences to reference over future distressing situations. This too shall pass in time.

## 57. Standing Up for Others

Advocating for vulnerable groups counters injustice through courageous integrity. Discuss ongoing biases certain populations face like ableism, racism or LGBTQ discrimination persisting locally and globally. Read diverse #OwnVoices literature illuminating varied experiences. Sign up families for equity training, then share conversation starters welcoming more marginalized friends into social circles. Report bigoted jokes immediately; explain historical pain provoked. Research civil rights youth leadership opportunities to uplift oppressed communities through mentoring/fundraising/political activism. Support identities embracing authentic selves. Protest harmful rhetoric alongsideImpact amplified by numbers. Whether everyday microaggressions or appalling atrocities occurring, pledging solidarity with targets prevents complicit bystanding when freedoms come under attack. Uniting against oppression lifts all of humanity.

## 58. Taking Responsibility

Marking maturity, accepting culpability for errors and oversights builds trust in relationships personal through professional. Explain judgment lapses often trace back to hurried overlooked details, not blatant disregard or spite. Demonstrate accountability through direct apologies, changed behaviors over time and restorative measures addressing impacts of mistakes rather than excuses covering uncomfortable truths. Discuss workplace ethics requiring reporting colleagues' dangerous negligence, employers' discrimination/harassment or products liability despite stigma risk as whistleblowers. Outline reasonable boundaries over sons' household duties but praise rather than scold consequential spill cleanups. Lead by mirroring responsible adulthood everything from waking on time, avoiding intoxication hazards to paying bills before recreation. Fortunes can turn suddenly, so build reputations withstanding hard times.

## 59. Caring for Pets

Assuming pet care responsibilities enhances empathy, compassion and planning habits necessary collaborating respectfully across species protecting animal welfare. Select developmentally-appropriate starter pets together like sea monkeys, hermit crabs up towards cats/dogs matching energy levels and space constraints. Vet adoption candidates thoroughly ensure temperaments mesh safely with family. Calculate considerable lifetime costs beforehand: supplies, veterinary needs and accommodations when traveling. Establish household policies about humane handling. Sign volunteer hour pledges at shelters to reinforce duties. Invest ample time socializing new pets through gentle cuddles, enrichment toys keeping powerful bite/scratch reflexes dormant and calming essential oil diffusers preventing destructive anxiety. If children ever lose capability to attend creature needs, guide responsible rehoming not abandons. Welcome furry friends!

## *60. Using the Internet Safely*

The internet delivers boundless knowledge when navigated prudently. Instill savvy filtering skills dismissing online misinformation and scams. Secure devices against hacking with antivirus software/firewalls and password protect accounts using symbols/phrases avoiding pet names easily discovered on social media. Set strict privacy settings defaulting away from public visibility. Steer clear of inflammatory communication breeding contention without context like emoji reactions or one-star reviews. Customize parental controls limiting screen time and enforcing safe search filters over concerning content. Share examples of photoshopped images warping perceptions around unrealistic beauty standards. Promote cyberbullying interventions protecting peers. The web presents limitless possibilities for those entering informed against preventable hazards.

## 61. Staying Safe Around Strangers

Unfortunately, dangerous strangers sometimes target vulnerable populations including children out alone getting groceries, walking after activities or lost appearing confused. Combat naivety without instilling excessive paranoia heightening anxiety disorders. Teach identifying subtle predatory grooming tactics used gaining cooperation like pretending authority positions, flattering compliments, bribing treats, needing directions assistance or feigning emergencies requiring violations of physical contact. Stress ignoring interactions from strangers, especially adults without other kids present. Report alarming behaviors like lingering stares, invasive questions or repeatedly circling perimeters near playgrounds/young clusters. Always walk in pairs after dark and stand away from cars offering rides.

Stay safe without forgoing cautious optimism. Most people hold kind intentions.

## 62. Using Proper Grammar

Correct grammar enables effective communication delivering messages clearly across diverse audiences. While creative shorthands like emoji strings possess playful utility between friends, succeeding academically and professionally relies on proper usages avoiding unintended meanings. Outline sentence part functions from subjects to verbs to descriptors. Define common mistakes like their/there/they're or too/two/to keep examples posted by workstations visualizing differences. Play Mad Lib grammar games injecting silly responses practicing parts of speech variations. Gently note family dialect speech patterns tied to regional upbringings rather than judging intelligence. Access free grammar helpers supplied by word processing tools.

Getting in habit prevents later retraining struggles to meet position needs valuing eloquent writing.

# Being a Positive Influence

## 63. Channeling Personal Hardships into Helping Others

Turn stumbling blocks into stepping stones uplifting communities through activism service. Applying familiarity with grief, discrimination or uncertainty often won through personal insight makes compassionate, approachable advocates. Consider which youth-led movements inspire injustices left unaddressed by previous generations like LGBTQ rights, gun violence prevention or accessible neighborhood playground construction benefiting children with disabilities. Schedule informational interviews to scope local needs from area nonprofits. Volunteer processing crisis hotline calls, sorting food pantry donations or beautifying parks alongside those utilizing services to humanize struggles. Fundraise selling homemade friendship bracelets or baked goods supporting beloved causes. Better yet, invite those with firsthand issue expertise to collaboratively lead awareness campaigns as equal partners instead of speaking on behalf of others. Helping others heals thyself.

## 64. Seeing Other Perspectives

Wisdom emerges understanding multifaceted viewpoints shaping complex human dynamics before responding thoughtfully. Practice shifting frames of reference across varied standpoints to envision alternate realities beyond your own dominant cultural experiences. For historical events, consider the same situations through opposing soldiers' patriotic convictions fighting rivals rather than enemies. Regard business developments playing executive roles concerned with companies' survival and livelihoods for many families despite environmental destruction allegations protested by activists. Over interpersonal conflicts, ask clarifying questions revealing hidden sensitivities like recent losses secretly grieved or financial constraints adding job pressures. Withholding reactive judgments unless walking miles through the shoes of others deepens empathy transforming conflict into connection.

## 65. Admitting When You're Wrong

Maturity manifests acknowledging mistakes when provided credible evidence contradicting stubborn stances, despite embarrassment swallowing pride initially. Model self-acceptance verbally untangling errors like misheard directions, inadvertent planning meeting oversights and forgotten relatives' birthdays as examples. Spotlight respected public figures throughout history who reversed earlier problematic positions after enlightening personal encounters, like George Wallace eventually renouncing segregation. Outline a framework for sincerely admitting wrongdoing: Thank the informant, apologize for impacts affected, explain causes behind the inaccurate viewpoint, offer to make amends, share takeaways improving responses next time and request patience rebuilding trustworthiness. Holding oneself accountable when entitled to deflect blame builds integrity.

## 66. Becoming More Accepting of Differences

Open-mindedness creates welcoming communities where all diverse members thrive feeling respected, understood and safe to express authentic identities freely without silencing marginalization. Combat unconscious "othering" within families through exposure expanding worldviews. Attend cultural festivals, befriend neighbors of varied backgrounds, read #OwnVoices literature from authors sharing protagonist demographics, sample international cuisine markets and follow activist social media accounts uplifting frequently misrepresented groups. Address insensitive speech immediately as learning opportunities even if unintentional; make amends redirecting future behavior positively. Though balancing differences inevitably causes occasional discord, celebrate this richness strengthening bonds beyond surface variances to find shared common ground in our collective humanity.

### 67. Comforting Others in Need

Lending emotional support during turbulent times provides stability when overwhelmed bearing burdens alone. Sharpen intuition reading body language, asking thoughtful questions and listening fully to uncover hidden hurts including grief, job loss grief and health diagnoses grief. Avoid platitudes rushing distressed individuals towards happiness before they process complex feelings themselves. Absorb anger outbursts resiliently rather than taking reactions personally. When professional counseling requires above skill levels, research referrals through health insurance coverage. Uplift other community pillars as needed consoling emotional pains. Simple consistent caring through homemade meals delivered, playful pet visits and solidarity sitting together wordlessly signals, "You are not alone. I am here." Healing happens through emotional connection.

# Doing Well in School:

## 68. Studying Efficiently

Maximize academic results without burning out. Tailor techniques suiting needs: Steady paced rereading to cement foundational knowledge, summarizing key concepts verbally to classmates, drawing colorful visual mnemonic devices interconnecting ideas, covering study guides through recordings replayed during chore routines, acing multiple choice tests through online quiz apps with instant results to check retention, collaborating with peers reviewing using classroom whiteboards...and so on. The secret lies in identifying fruitless activities producing little measurable progress after timed trials. If desperate late night cramming consistently fails come exam periods, reassess counterproductive habits. Perhaps simply reviewing difficult materials routinely in smaller chunks rather than prolonged all-at-once marathons proves more successful without exhausting focus. Stay open trying evidence-based strategies maximizing individual absorption rates.

## 69. *Getting Along with Teachers*

Like any relationship, student-teacher connections significantly impact happiness and effectiveness in academic environments. Set positive tones early each term introducing yourselves and asking preferred classroom management styles supporting optimal learning. Treat instructors respectfully as colleagues rather than adversaries, especially regarding disagreements. Express genuine interest about subjects taught, compliment innovative presentations, send thank you notes after support during struggles and give grace around inevitable overwhelmed days managing many priorities from families to faculty politics. Should tensions escalate beyond peaceful repairs, discretely request equitable mediators clarifying misunderstandings before destructive assumptions cement permanently. Ideal classrooms uplift through inspiration, not fear or favoritism. Everyone deserves feeling safe to learn without judgment.

### 70. Avoiding Gossip

Reputational damage and peer alienation often result from participating in gossip perceiving everything heard as absolute fact rather than questioning the accuracy of information or motivation of the teller. Stop conversational rumors immediately by declining to entertain unverified accounts. Stress feeling uncomfortable spreading potential misinformation or contributing to tensions between others. Direct peers with serious concerns to initiate private constructive meetings allowing accused individuals opportunities clarifying truths before groups rush shaming judgments. Encourage assuming positive intentions in most cases unless assessing repeated patterns indicating more sinister behaviors across multiple low risk situations. While anonymity breeds gossip's dangerous influential power online especially, in real world school settings accountability traces back sources directly hence wisdom cautiously pausing to verify details before propagating claims based on he said/she said alone.

## 71. Knowing When to Get Involved

Witnessing interpersonal student conflicts brings grueling choices between intervening directly at personal risk to prevent immediate harm, escalating issues further or alerting responsible authorities as mandated reporters, especially regarding discrimination and assaults. Recognize underlying dynamics like long term bully patterns, power imbalances, vulnerabilities requiring advocacy if asking targeted peers directly only fuels retaliation fears silencing them more. Collect evidence discreetly then act decisively making formal reports to ensure thorough investigations as due process allows all sides sharing evidence before conclusions finalize. Emphasize grave effects bullying inflicts through stress-related disabilities and suicide risks when initially downplayed left unattended too long over months or years while tension secretly festers. Standing by doing nothing signals passive approval granting dangerous behaviors continued access thriving unchecked and growing bolder harming more over time.

## 72. Improving Your Focus

Distractions disrupt learning, especially in phases of life that are saturated with technology and driven by busy routines. You can strengthen your concentration through gamified apps, like Lazer Mazer or Elevate. These apps build memory, planning, and processing speeds through short, repetitive activities that can be integrated between other commitments. Use online focus timers like Forest blocking screens during duration limits set. Take scheduled sensory breathers during lengthy study sessions rather than multitasking through social media, restoring fatigued directed attention spans crashing after an hour or so uninterrupted. populate workspaces with fidget tools like Velcro strips under desks, finger labyrinths tracing during lectures or adjoining sketch journals drawing concept connections fluidly. Request front row seating minimizing external stimuli in direct eye lines. Sharpen mental clarity maximizing potential through neuroplasticity deliberately training minds growing increasingly distracted yet desperately competitive focus-wise.

## 73. Working on Difficult Subjects

All students face academically weaker skill areas needing improvement meeting graduation requirements and career prospects. Before tensions peak, develop game plans itemizing personalized obstacles to conquer through school and public resources. Seek tutoring early in struggles, even preemptively shoring up challenges predicted by prior years' trends. Appeal any test accommodations legally entitled if applicable like readers, scribes, separate testing rooms or added time allotments. Schedule periodic check-ins with counselors mapping incremental progress during the term. Dissect broad deficiencies into comprehensible steps completed systematically. Perhaps mastering double digit multiplication builds towards more complex calculus operations later. Meet with department teachers mapping supplemental summer curriculums bridging gaps cheaper than repeat credits required if failing badly come final grades. Align electives engaging natural strengths elevating weaker topics. Small gains accumulate if persisting patiently.

## 74. Retaining What You Learn

Memorization strategies aid long term content retention automatically accessed during high pressure academic testing environments when tension freezes minds drawing blanks. To input memorable mnemonic devices creatively connect intangible facts through concrete physical anchor concepts using acronyms, sayings, props, songs or stories. Pepper educational games into studying through trivia apps testing recall speed linking correct responses. Make pop quizzes mimicking classroom scenarios including racing timers adding urgency. Draw diagram concept maps noting interconnected relationship flows. Apply content directly teaching someone else without notes on call to check durable absorption. The more senses engaged with material through models manipulated, debates argued aloud instead of only reading silently again and again, the higher details stick becoming readily available for smooth retrievals.

## 75. Earning Good Grades

Beyond gauging topic mastery, strong academic performances grant students privileged opportunities like awards, advanced classes and recommendation letters required to access competitive colleges or career paths afterwards. Devise a customizable formula calculating raw numerical averages needed for each desired letter benchmark whether aiming high towards honors societies or just passing while juggling obligations outside academics like family jobs. Calculate estimated points per assignments by category percentages as quarter or semester outlooks. Build graduated scaffold supports preventing issues escalating into irreparable situations jeopardizing wider goals. With an emphasis on outcomes rather than comparing against peers' with less equivalent circumstances, empower students feeling in control of destinies through self-advocacy, focused responses to feedback addressing deficiencies identified by instructors promptly and shifting habits when conventional methods repeatedly yield unsatisfactory results warranting new ideas before prospects narrow from closing enrollment dates for desirable next chapter options.

## 76. Speaking Confidently in Class

Public speaking skills translate valuable beyond academia into professional and civic community leadership capacities. While class participation anxiety endures as a widespread phobia, behavioral conditioning techniques build vocal confidence incrementally through role plays, volunteer responses when comfortable occasionally daily and inhaling empowering aroma scents from essential oils. Set small speaking goals first. Perhaps reading aloud paragraphs from novels rather than summarizing understandings initially. Vocal volume and eye contact further develop through quick check-in reading partners sharing a few sentences summarizing homework just completed the previous night to drill frequently without excessive spotlight pressures. Later lead groups presented completed projects incorporating multimedia technology props staying conversant alongside verbal talking points. Eventually passion naturally engages spontaneous interactions. With compassion, patience yourself and peers deliver content compellingly.

## 77. Coping with Sadness and Loss

Navigating grief while maintaining school responsibilities challenges resiliency. Validate mourning processes respectfully after death losses or romantic breakups processing traumatic experiences through stages including denial, yearning, anger, sadness before reaching acceptance. Encourage journaling, creative arts therapies, sports and letting tears flow freely. Refer counseling if needed. Discuss spiritual questions brought up pondering existence's meaning. When grades slip post-loss, collaborate with teachers arranging accommodations until regaining capacities. Expect memory/concentration impairment symptoms immediately after too. Offer flexible attendance options if family leave gets denied or students feel isolated staying home alone instead. However, balance leniencies expecting substantial effort displayed still when present applying themselves. Healing happens slowly. Explain depression warning signs requiring urgent care should darkness persist without improvements concerning durations. This too shall pass with support.

## 78. Completing Assignments Honestly

Cheating consequences often outweigh perceived shortcuts gained dishonestly through plagiarism or forbidden collaborating hiding individual knowledge gaps. Acknowledge temptation rationalizations in high stakes grading environments tied to competitive opportunities. Outline alternative outcomes bolstering integrity through authentic skill development even if temporarily earning lower scores. Differentiate harmless group studying from flagrant copying answer keys online boards night before major testing. Require citing helper names on projects. Address underlying motivations directly rather than reactively punishing isolated incidents alone falling short upholding academic ethics completely moving forwards. If anxiety-fueled over compensation stems from perfectionist pressure more than entitlement, decrease external stressors and practice slower paced self-care habits preventing recurring dishonest reactions flaring up again. Uphold personal honor codes elevating character protecting reputations long run.

## 79. Understanding Plagiarism

Plagiarism steals authorship credit from original thinkers dedicating efforts creating intellectual property freely benefitting audiences through published conduit mediums. While technology enables quick cutting/pasting digital bits reshuffled conveniently supporting arguments without proper citations credits earlier minds laying that groundwork, such deception intends advancing personal gains like grades dishonestly off others dedicated labor. Beyond moral reasons upholding justice, significant practical repercussions justify teaching this critical topic. Reputations determine careers built through renowned expertise boasting extensive catalogs showing influential leadership spearheading change through ethical research contributions valued by companies, academia and social movements alike needing proven trustworthiness credentials verified not violating past rules before risking future stakes appointing key roles with increased influence responsibilities going forwards especially when visibility spotlights magnify exponentially. Therefore establish vigilant personal accountability standards early preventing external allegations questioning integrity later.

## Working Outdoors Safely:

### 80. Washing Cars Properly

Washing automobiles responsibly prevents environmental runoff hazards from entering watersheds. Select biodegradable cleaners avoiding phosphate concentrates promoting algae choking out marine life. Restrict usage minimizing needed amounts using pressure settings without wasting excess. Divert drainage towards grassy slopes and gravel beds filtering gradually instead of straight into storm sewers. Sample runoff ensures neutral pH levels before releasing. Focus rinses on muddiest sections preventing broader spreading across wider areas. Dispose of filthy buckets properly rather than dumping casually curbside flowing eventually to sewers after next rains. Handle solvent containers cautiously avoiding spills through firmly sealed lids and storage far from flood risks in locked garages or sheds. Model conscientious car care protecting community water supplies sustaining healthy future generations and ecosystems alike.

## 81. Maintaining Vehicles

Performing basic preventative maintenance vastly extends automobile lifespans preventing minor issues compounding into major mechanical nightmares stranding mobility suddenly. Follow factory recommended schedules inspecting belts, brakes, filters, fluid levels, lights, tire treads and wheel alignments every six months or set mileage intervals. Tackle oil/filter changes, battery load testing and brake pad replacements during seasonal transitions checking off each spring/fall checklist noting future deadline forecasts. Maintain detailed logs documenting parts replacements, damage repairs, tune ups and deep cleaning dates as caring histories should vehicles transfer ownership throughout life cycles. Washing exteriors regularly prevents corrosion and waxy build ups; vacuuming interiors maintains resale values for eventual trade ins. Handle all repairs promptly yourself or through trusted mechanics. Don't take transportation access for granted!

## 82. Practicing Safety Around Cars

Traffic injuries devastate millions of families annually worldwide. Statistically highest vehicle related causes link to distracted driving, impaired reactions, excessive speeding and improperly restrained occupants. Eliminate cell phone handling, rowdy passengers loud noises and complex navigation systems diverting eyes off the road and hands grasping wheels steady. Plan buffer travel time preparing for unexpected delays preventing temptation accelerating riskily chronic lateness. Secure all contents avoiding dangerous projectiles through collisions. Confirm everyone wears seat belts or properly installed child restraints suitable for sizes/weights. Adhere traffic signs/signals strictly; idle at crosswalks ensuring pedestrian clearance before proceeding turns noting surroundings vigilantly avoiding smaller cyclists and playing children hidden from average sightlines when taller vehicles surround just like school bus monitors trained professionally emphasize observing dangers directly. Driving deserves undivided attention protecting all lives sharing interconnected mobility spaces.

## 83. Mowing Lawns Correctly

Power mowers cause over 400,000 emergency injuries annually for consumers in North America alone according to U.S. Consumer Product Safety Commission data. Heed caution operating machinery equipped with sharp spinning blades slicing through dense growth capable of puncturing sturdy shoes if accidentally slipped underfoot catching toeports while hands stabilizing heavy frames lose grip falling. Expect flying gravel, insects and natural debris discharged through discharge chutes too. Wear certified steel toed boots, protective eyeglasses, sturdy gloves and noise canceling over-ear defenders rating 20+ decibels NRR dampening against certain models measuring over 90 ear-piercing decibels equivalent to chainsaws or jet engines when listeners need protected proximity. Clean guards and shields keeping visibility unobstructed, monitoring turf conditions ahead rather than just dust clouds. Double check equally hazard zone proximity assuming pedestrians or pets stay remaining clear before beginning routines.

## 84. Handling Automotive Fluids Carefully

Oils, gasoline, transmission fluids and antifreeze contain toxic chemicals dangerous ingesting requiring careful handling during mechanical home garaging work. Review warning labels completely understanding exposure risks before usage storing appropriately sealed and locked preventing environmental spills entering watersheds or curious child access reaching stored containers left unsecured. Always wear gloves resistant against these solvent compounds when checking/refilling reservoirs. Clean drips immediately with proper absorbents like granulated clay cat litter, not water spreading slicks further. Allow cooled engines before unscrewing hot caps avoiding steam eruptions meeting faces. Requests help tilting awkward vehicles when accessing difficult underside compartments. Ventilate workspace areas thoroughly because prolonged vapor inhalation poses serious health consequences too. Take precautions seriously because these powerful automotive fluids enable transportation conveniences improving quality lives.

## 85. Identifying Dangerous Snakes

Herpetology surveys document over 3,000 snake species globally with approximately 20% packing potent venom delivering potentially fatal dosages through fangs and other auxiliary grooved teeth exposing prey tissue to fast-acting toxins triggering rapid immobilization and digestion. Of medically significant serpents in Americas, watch for triangular heads housing specialized structures suitable envenomation processes contrasted against non-venomous counterparts usually boasting smaller rounded snouts. Memorize local varieties based on color/pattern combinations using reliable digital field guides and note environments favored like aquatic zones near streams/lakes versus open grasslands overheated forcing cold-blooded creatures seeking shade. Teach appropriate snake safety instead of fear like providing pictures to children at safe distances appreciating ecological benefits pest control and stressing importance of leaving undisturbed because nearly all bites result in mishandled harassment. When in doubt, assume danger backing away slowly without sudden movements upsetting defensive reflex strikes.

## 86. Identifying Poisonous Plants

Many common backyard and wild plants contain skin-contact irritating oils in leaves, berries or sap. Teach identification techniques inspecting leaf arrangements opposite (across from each other) or alternate, identifiers like white sap, umbrella woody-like cluster stems clumped for poison ivy/oak/sumac, thorny rashes from nettles, fine stiff needle-like hairs delivering histamine-releasing chemicals into pores, bulb vegetables like onions triggering responses when brushing past and clustering mini fruits signaling nightshade family risks so realistically never snacking random samples without specialist guidance. When discovering skin redness, burning sensations, swelling or blisters appearing on exposed contact areas associated with recent woods adventures, clean with rubbing alcohol, cold water and topical hydrocortisone applications before deciding if further medical advice warrants depending on severity reaction levels. Stay vigilant since many botanicals camouflage stealthily along common trails waiting to brush past legs!

## 87. Staying Safe in Bad Weather

Storms bring unpredictable threats requiring preparedness minimizing dangers. Assess structural vulnerabilities like aged roofs/windows at risk during extreme winds or lightning strikes setting nearby flammable property alight. Stock emergency kits to survive independently several days lacking basic Grid services should they fail through fallen electrical poles or flooded municipal water facilities. Fill gas tanks allowing powered mobility if needed. Learn warning siren tones differentiating disaster types in your county since protocols vary responding to active shooters versus extreme weather events. Have a designated crowded interior room or basement ready without exterior touching walls for tornado safe sheltering. Avoid driving across water-covered roads measured deceptively deeper than tire heights stalling engines catastrophically. Set phones receiving advance alerts from trusted meteorologists. Lacking optimal choices, risk evaluations guide next survival steps rather than panic paralysis endangering further. Stay situationally aware!

## 88. Using Radios in Emergencies

Battery-powered AM/FM radios provide critical local news updates during regional power/cellular/internet outages associated with extreme weather disasters or infrastructure attacks. Stay alert tuning favorite stations rather than automatically streaming personalized playlists oblivious to escalating danger zones nearby. Silence mobile alerts allowing clear radio signal focus without endless lower priority interruptions delaying real-time instructions. Gather all family members within hearing range of broadcasting speakers to uniformly interpret announcements together. Boost signals optimally adjusting antenna angles narrowly targeting distant transmitter tower origins directly rather than indifferent arbitrary musical entertainment Craving borderline addiction habits plaguing wider culture. Amid chaos, calming NPR anchors accompany delivering possibly life saving advisories from governor declarations authorizing emergency resources towards boil water contamination warnings or missing loved ones reunification shelter points depending evolving aftermath needs. Disaster readiness assumes responsible communications hierarchy prioritizations.

## 89. Reading Maps

Map literacy fosters navigation independence, spatial awareness and mental curiosity about destinations near/far. Guide children interpreting colorful keys, scale ratios, cardinal directions, contour lines showing elevation changes and grid coordinate systems pinpointing locations exactly. Have them estimate mileage magnitudes between points tracking routes visually. Study highway maps before road trips identifying rest stops and estimating reasonable pace progressions. Geoguessr web and mobile games drop players randomly needing deducing placement based countryside clues scanned. Subscribe to atlases capturing their interests like fantasy realm cartographies from beloved book series. Spark lifelong learning through interactive maps profiling everything from oceanic shipwrecks, aviation no fly zones, historical battles and Michael Jordan's career shooting heat zones! Hard Copy paper maps withstand technology failures longer too unlike electric dependencies.The world unfolds exciting journeys however mapped!

## 90. Asking for Directions Safely

When disoriented in unfamiliar settings, humbly requesting guidance prevents mistaken assumptions worsening situations traveling further astray literally and metaphorically. However, sadly predators sometimes exploit perceptions targeting vulnerable persons like children separated from guardians. Before approaching strangers, assess body language intuition cues for benevolent intentions verbally and physically. Avoid isolated areas. Locate safer public places like stores where employees wear name tags accountable as representatives for behavioral complaints if needed. Have someone capture license plate numbers from a distance while interacting just in case. Politely disengage anyone probing personal questions insistently. Quickly call emergency contacts on cell phones kept sufficiently charged carrying exact addresses. Alternatively walk towards higher traffic intersections improving visibility drastically less likely perpetuating crimes under witnessing eyes. Ask while applying streetwise caution trusting vibes.

## Appearance and Hygiene:

### 91. Caring for Your Hair

Healthy hair results from gentle cleansing, thorough conditioning, protective styling, hydrating masks and occasional trims sustaining ends minimizing splits unraveling length faster through breakage. Massage botanical shampoos into scalps, not matted lengths risking over-sudsing tangled deep. Rinse thoroughly. Apply damaged-healing masques combating chlorine/saltwater dye processing damage when affordable. Explore diverse hair types' specific needs consulting licensed stylists, whether curl patterns warranting wide tooth combs minimizing frizz, processed tendencies requiring intensive keratin treatments or cultural practices incorporating nourishing oils passed down generations benefiting thicker textures. Handle gently towel drying or air drying minimally rubbing. Express yourself through fun colors when older yet know professional corrections prove pricey if dissatisfied certain shades against complexions later. Confidence beams beginning healthy hair days!

## 92. Styling Your Hair

Whether special occasion elegant updos, daily uniformity maintaining professionalism or personally expressive liberty spikes broadcasting alternative flair, experimenting new looks explores identity. Master usual routines first like neatly parted cornrow braids, undone messy buns for casual Fridays or slicked backed gelled styles sticking through hours of activities without embarrassing collapsing reveals. Incorporate accessories like embellished clips, preppy headbands or vintage scarves. Ask trusted hairdressers attempting technical tricks beyond current skill levels like balayage ombre, precision undercuts or corrective coloring mishaps avoided without proper foil placements. Attending industry hair shows widening inspirations. Schedule occasional blowouts treating yourself. Consult teens sincerely before significantly altering lengths that took years growing, as peer perceptions painfully affect fragile adolescent stages already challenging enough. Enjoy tasteful transformations suiting settings.

## 93. Planning Outfits

Harmonious aesthetics projects put together impressions through coordinating colors, patterns and proportional silhouettes suiting body types. Guide age-appropriate selections not overemphasizing physical appearances yet positively enhancing natural beauty everyone inherently possesses. Suggest classic capsule wardrobes with versatile essential pieces mixing/matching multiple outfits spinning endless combinations suitable occasions from creative casual Fridays sartorial freedom to formal winter ball elegance exuding sophistication. Share sealing tricks like color wheel complementary hues, anchor necklaces drawing outfit cohesion and seasonal layering expanding transitional wear during shoulder seasons between extremes. Encourage individual statements like bold shoe choices while preventing inappropriate extremes clashing environments like tap shoes crackling libraries. Ensure properly fitted apparel avoiding structural discomfort. Appropriate presentations make lasting favorable first impressions.

## 94. Caring for Your Skin

PubertyWelcome changing complexions compassionately without magnifying self-consciousness since comparisons prove unconstructive. Arm teens against intensified oil production creating acne with medicated cleansers staying gentle avoiding inflammation worsening breakouts. Hydrate scaling dry patches trying oils first before resulting prescriptions. Prevent skin cancer risks by applying broad spectrum SPF 30+ sunblocks daily, more so for paler pigments burning faster. Tan "safely" in reputable salons rather than risking DNA damage through blistering peeling agony by ignorant overexposing attempting quick tropical looks unsupervised. Recommend dermatology specialists sooner than later restoring clarity avoiding permanent scarring if aggressive cysts require medical treatments beyond over the counter product promises. Confidence radiates fairest complexions equally as deepest melanated rich tones when caring properly.

## 95. Using Sun Protection

Ultraviolet radiation exponentially increases skin cancer risks through accumulated exposure intensity. Defend vigorously against threat. Seek shade whenever possible during peak intensity hours around solar noon. Wear wide brimmed hats, tightly woven long sleeves and UPF clothing blocking rays better unlike regular fabrics transmitting through pores. Apply broad spectrum SPF 30+

water-resistant sunblocks liberally exposed areas every 80 minutes minimum because light beams still penetrate and degrade protection layers faster through sweating, rubbing or swimming activities. Reapply eyelid skin thinner than others. Store medications properly avoiding high interior temperature damage compromising expected protections. Know skin cancer visual warning signs involving pigmentation irregularities, reddish scaly rough patches and raised bleeding moles changing abruptly by appearances or sensations. Schedule annual dermatology screenings monitoring concerning developments aggressively early before malignance spreads deeper and impossible stopping. Prevention works!

## 96. Dressing Appropriately

Social conventions dictate dress codes indicating situational respect. Attire meeting contextual expectations conveys consideration while flagrant defiance risksRelationships. Advise school uniforms begrudgingly imposed eliminating classist competition among peers. Suggest interview outfits erring more formal than underwhelming. Redirect daring self-expression violating formal venue expectations better celebrated elsewhere. Pack attire suiting anticipated weather, activities and impromptu invitations navigating uncertainty. Discuss cultural appropriation regarding adopting aesthetic expressions without consent or contexts. Guide semi-formal wear rentals avoiding costly purchases outgrowing quickly. During identity explorations playfully push comfort zones through edgy accessories rather than permanent tattoos later regretted. Ultimately emphasize clothing selections reflecting inner character virtues making lasting honorable impressions beyond superficial judging books by covering clichés that historically marginalized top talent nevertheless. Model adaptable humility remaining curious asking clarifying questions more than complaining.

## 97. Ironing Clothes

Wrinkled wrinkled clothing broadcasts disorganization dimming credible first impressions often needed through professional or formal settings. Proficient ironing saves expensive dry cleaning bills over time. Assemble essential equipment like spray bottles lightly moistening garment fibers smoothing easier once heated tools make contact. Use adjustable ironing boards lowering heights ergonomically for young learners avoiding back strains late growth spurts bring. Select appropriate heat settings compatible fabric material types indicated on permanent tags. Glide slowly applying firm even pressure smoothing entire wrinkled surfaces, not skipping around haphazardly lingering too long scorching holes ultimately absolutely ruining items damaged if distracted multitasking other household chores simultaneously while waiting. Follow straight grain lines from top shoulder seams towards hemlines lifting creases efficiently finished quicker than struggling against weave threads unnecessarily. Crisp precision ironing mastery levels up style games effortlessly elevating overall presentation polish eloquently.

## 98. Finding Personal Style

External presentations symbolically reflect inner world self-perceptions whether consciously intentionally defined or unintentionally perceived by others when observing aesthetic embodiment displays. Guide exploring emerging personal styles genuinely representing dynamic character developments seeking truths within. Master fundamentals first properly fit flattering classics aligning positive external feedback building confidence slowly going forwards next expressing bolder incarnations like dyeing hair rainbow colors matching quirky mannerisms or tattooing poetic verses displaying compassionately on forearms constantly volunteering giving humble service silently expecting zero recognition in return. Compare attempts sincerely assessing what worked against criticisms identifying growth adjustments better aligning values with updated looks. Recognize self-expression constantly evolves through ever-changing size bodies, maturity perspectives and identity phases seeking alignments no longer resonating with past versions once resonated before necessarily. Stay patient loving yourself along journeys less criticizing delighting full acceptance where presently stand today.

## 99. Brushing and Flossing Teeth

Consistent oral healthcare prevents painful tooth decay and exorbitant dental expenses accruing as problems compound without early minimally invasive interventions. Guide proper techniques brushing gently massaging gums two minutes twice daily using soft bristle or electric toothbrushes with ADA-approved fluoride concentrations strengthening enamel defenses against acidic biofilm attacks. Floss daily disrupts further buildup between tight teeth cavities otherwise impossible reaching effectively through bristles alone no matter how slender designed or diligently wielded. Rinse using antimicrobial mouthwash killing remaining germs lingering MICRO spaces. Schedule professional cleanings every 6 months removing stubborn calculus deposits through specialized scaling tools and powerful suction wands impossible duplicating without industry experience. When affordable, protect against bites wearing custom fitted night guards preventing destructive grinding/clenching habits developing micro fractures exponentially costlier fixing later through crowns, implants or orthodontics! Prevention sustains healthy beautiful smiles.

## 100. Feeling Good about How You Look

Positive body images greatly improve mental health and interpersonal connections. Guide children seeing their existing beauty without magnifying artificial physical "flaws" warped by unrealistic media standards digitally altering appearances setting harmful expectations almost no one attains unedited. Share your personal self-acceptance journey overcoming insecure comparisons or societal barriers dismissively judging attributes like skin conditions, disability mobility aids and non-binary gender expressions all equally deserving embracing dignity. Discuss how personalities, creative talents and kindness quotients far outweigh appearances despite looks wielding unjust influence still today. As adolescents explore identity experiments trying temporary style phases, focus critiques on what flatters individuals already rather than chasing hypothetical ideals impersonally marketed rather than celebrating personal uniqueness diversity. Confidence builds positive momentum gradually through supportive mirrors reflecting back beloved truths.

## 101. Building Confidence in Yourself

Construct unshakable self-assurance foundations uplifting potential fearlessly pursuing passions productively without awaiting outside validation perpetually conditional upon meeting others' agendas. Identify innate strengths and proven competencies demonstrated through past wins small and large. Catalog steady accumulation milestones quantifying exponential career/character developments over decades. Recognize imposter syndrome false humility patterns underselling experiential credentials devaluing expert insight gifts contributing benefiting communities, industries and movements when shared courageously. Visualize futures capitalizing capabilities aligned values empowering greater good. Write encouragement notes rebutting inner saboteurs seeking to protect comfort zones rather than champions destining unlimited growth beyond barriers that no longer serve highest selves. You contain every resource necessary manifesting destinies awaiting activated brave belief unlocking highest self actualization now.

# ABOUT THE AUTHOR

**Katherine Santos** is an accomplished parent, educator, and a published author specializing in the field of psychology, relationship and parenting. With a wealth of expertise, she has authored highly acclaimed books including Rage Management for Parents, A beginners handbook on parenting children with ADHD and Life Skills for Teens, Romantic relationships, Self-help and so on.

With an unwavering commitment to the study of psychology spanning over 25 years, Katherine has focused extensively on childhood development and effective parenting strategies. Her dedication to this field drives her mission to assist others in successfully navigating the challenges that arise in the realm of parenting.

Drawing from her extensive educational background and firsthand experiences as a mother of four children (comprising two boys and two girls), Katherine has developed a holistic approach that caters to parents, teenagers, and children from diverse backgrounds. Her deep understanding of psychology, combined with practical parenting insights, ensures that her guidance is accessible and beneficial to individuals from all walks of life.

*Katherine Santos* is your trusted source for expert guidance in the intricate world of parenting and child development